NUMBER FORTY-SEVEN

IN THE SERIES OF KEEPSAKES

ISSUED BY

THE FRIENDS OF THE BANCROFT LIBRARY

FOR ITS MEMBERS

Mark Twain, September 1872.

Mark Twain
Press Critic

Two previously unpublished essays

by Mark Twain

Interviewing the Interviewer

and

The American Press

༈

Commentary by

Thomas C. Leonard

University Librarian and Professor of Journalism

The Friends of The Bancroft Library
University of California at Berkeley
2003

DESIGNED AND PRINTED BY AÑO NUEVO ISLAND PRESS.

CONTENTS

Illustrations

Mark Twain on 12 September 1872,
photographed by W. and A. H. Fry, Brighton, England.
(Mark Twain's Letters, Volume 5, p. 652)

frontispiece

Mark Twain on 14 or 16 November 1874,
photographed by George Kendall Warren, Boston.
(Mark Twain's Letters, Volume 6, pp. 302-3)

page 10

Mark Twain, center, pictured with fellow journalists
George Alfred Townsend and David Gray. Photographed by
Mathew Brady on 7 February 1871, Washington D.C.
(Mark Twain's Letters, Volume 4, p. 571)

page 12

The first two pages from the manuscript of "Interviewing the
Interviewer." Mark Twain has carefully styled the typeface for the
title and indicated in the top left corner that it was his intended
weekly contribution to the Buffalo *Express*.
Original manuscript in the Mark Twain Papers,
The Bancroft Library.

pages 18, 19

Two pages from near the end of the 13-page manuscript of
"The American Press," written between June and September 1888.
Original manuscript in the Mark Twain Papers,
The Bancroft Library.

pages 26, 27

Mark Twain, November 1874.

Mark Twain, Press Critic
by Thomas C. Leonard

EACH TIME THAT THE BANCROFT LIBRARY goes to press with the unpublished words of Mark Twain, it is evening the score with this American master. Mark Twain thought that libraries were taking advantage of him, killing sales of his stories by circulating them for free. He did not foresee that The Bancroft Library—active even in his lifetime—would go to the great trouble of making it possible to read his mind a century later.

Here are pieces of Mark Twain's mind in his lifelong worry over the American press. Samuel Clemens entered the printer's trade when he was 13 and by the time he grew into the pen name, Mark Twain, at 27, he had met many newspaper deadlines both in setting type and reporting news. Literature was to make his fortune (libraries did not really cut his book royalties). But writing for newspapers such as the Virginia City (Nevada) Territorial Enterprise *and the San Francisco* Alta California *first made his name. He settled into married life as an owner and editor of the Buffalo (New York)* Express. *His friendship with powerful Americans such as General Ulysses S. Grant took him into the newspaper wars of the Gilded Age. So Mark Twain knew first hand what the American press could do. He frequently erupted in outrage, more rarely praise, throughout his long life of news reading.*

You hold in your hands one of Mark Twain's curses on journalists and also his moving praise. The essays have never been published before. Their historical context is important, of course, but you do not need to know what was provoking Mark Twain in the winter of 1870 and the summer of 1888 to enjoy the roll of his words. Take a holiday from fairness; hear Mark Twain out.

GEORGE ALFRED TOWNSEND, MARK TWAIN, AND DAVID GRAY, PHOTOGRAPHED BY MATHEW BRADY, FEBRUARY 1871.

Interviewing
The Interviewer

I FOUND THE EDITOR of the New York *Sun* throned in his sanctum. He had his brimless cap on—his thinking cap, he terms it, and well he may, for many an exquisite fancy has it hatched out in its time. He was steeped in meditation. He was arranging in his mind a series of those articles for his next day's paper which have made the *Sun* famous in the land and a welcome visitor in every cultivated home circle upon the continent—interesting murders, with all the toothsome particulars; libels upon such men and women as have deserved the attention by being prominently blameless; aggravated cases of incest, with improving and elevating details; prize fights, elucidated with felicitously descriptive technicalities; elaborate histories of executions, assassinations and seductions; zealous defences of Reddy the Blacksmith and other persecuted patrons of the *Sun* who chance to stumble into misfortune. A high and noble thing it is to be the chief editor of a great metropolitan two-cent journal and mould the opinions of the washerwomen and achieve the applause of the bone and sinew of the back streets and the cellars. And when that editor is gifted with that endowment which we term Genius, verily his position is almost godlike. I felt insignificant in the company of Charles A. Dana—and who wouldn't?

I said:

"Sir, I am a stranger to you, but being a journalist in a small way myself, I have presumed upon this fellowship to intrude upon you, and beg, at the fountain-head of

American journalism, for a few little drops of that wisdom which has enabled you to confer splendor upon a profession which groped in darkness till your *Sun* flamed above its horizon."

"Be seated, sir, be seated. Ask what you will—I am always ready to instruct the ignorant and inexperienced."

"To come at once to the point, and not rob of their intellectual sustenance the suffering millions of our countrymen who hang upon your editorials, I desire to know the secret of your success—I desire to know what course one must pursue in order to make the name of his paper a household word at every fireside and a necessity unto all creatures whose idea of luxury soars to the equivalent of two cents."

"My son, unto none but you would I reveal the secret. You have paid me the homage which the envious multitude of so-called journalists deny me, and you shall be rewarded. Let the others suffer. Listen. The first great end and aim of journalism is to make a *sensation*. Never let your paper go to press without a sensation. If you have none, make one. Seize upon the prominent events of the day, and clamor about them with a maniacal fury that shall compel attention. Vilify everything that is unpopular—harry it, hunt it, abuse it, without rhyme or reason, so that you get a sensation out of it. Laud that which is popular—unless you feel sure that you can make it unpopular by attacking it. Hit every man that is down—never fail in this, for it is safe. Libel every man that can be ruined by it. Libel every prominent man who dare not soil his hands with touching you in return. But glorify all moneyed scum and give columns of worship unto the monuments they erect in honor of themselves, for moneyed men will not put up with abuse from small newspapers. If an uncalled-for onslaught upon a neighboring editor who has made you play second fiddle in journalism can take the bread out of his mouth and send him in disgrace from his post, let him have it! Do not mind a little lying, a liberal garbling of his telegrams, a mean prying into his private affairs and a pitiful and treacherous exposure of his private letters. It takes a very small nature to get down to this, but I managed it, and you can—and it makes a princely sensation. If two prominent preachers solemnize a questionable deathbed marriage when custom does not require them to cipher at the rights of the case until it is too late and one of the parties dies, go for them! Make fiends of them! Howl, and gnash your teeth, and rave with virtuous indignation till you convince yourself that in spite of your native rottenness you have some of the raw material of a saint in you, after all. But if those preachers *refuse* to solemnize the marriage, and go driveling around after information till the bridegroom dies and the bride goes crazy, *then* you can howl with fortyfold power about the soulless inhumanity of those divines. Simply a little change of base and you can make it appear that nothing is so damnable as the spectacle of a preacher refusing a deathbed request of any kind for any reason whatsoever."

[*Enter a Reporter.*]

"Mr. D., there is a report that Gen. Grant was drunk yesterday."

"Is there any truth in it?"

"No, sir."

"Then publish it by all means—say it *is* true—make a sensation of it—invent affidavits."

[*Exit Reporter.*]

"Yes, my son, in journalism, the idea is to deal in injurious personalities as much as you can, but you must make it a point to pitch into the helpless—it is the safest course. Make yourself a sort of Ishmael; have no friendships that are worthy; praise nothing that is worthy of praise; hate everything that other men love; cackle your opinions upon all subjects and upon all occasions with a swaggering pretense that the people attach weight to them; delve among forbidden subjects and revel among their filth, for it is the life of a two-cent paper; uncover all rapes and seductions, and expose them to the public gaze. In a word, be shameless—have this virtue and you need no other to make a two-cent paper succeed. And as soon as success is achieved, the illustrated papers will print your picture and publish your startlingly eventless biography, written by yourself."

[*Enter a Reporter.*]

"Mr. D., Gen. W. is dead."

"Ah, that is fortunate. A dangerous man—a very dangerous man. But now we can settle with him. Write an abusive obituary, and traduce the character of his mother."

"And Mr. Greeley has fallen on the ice and hurt himself seriously."

"Ah, that is fortunate also. State that he was under the influence of liquor. I wish we could do something to make the *Tribune* notice us."

[*Exit Reporter.*]

"Another feature, my son, is the interviewing business. We used to do a good thing in that line, but latterly *Sun* reporters find it difficult to get access to respectable people. However, it matters little. We seldom printed what people actually said, anyhow, and so we can get up the interviews just as well in the office as elsewhere. Try your hand at it— I think you will like it. Journalism, my son, is a great business—a very great business—and I feel that I do not flatter myself when I say that I have made of the New York *Sun* an entirely unique paper—nothing like it ever existed before, out of perdition. It is a wonderful newspaper. And I could have made just such a one out of that Chicago

Republican if they had let me stay, but that story they got up there about my having an improper intimacy with the aged chief of police angered me to such a degree that I would not remain. The whole city regretted my departure, and so did the newspaper men. The papers published kindly and appreciative farewells, and some of them were very touching. One paper published a long and flattering biography of me, and said in conclusion: 'We deeply regret the departure of this gifted writer from our midst. We have seen meaner men than him—we have seen much meaner men than Charles A. Dana—though we cannot recall an instance just now.' For the first time in many years I shed tears when I read that article."

[*Enter a Reporter.*]

"Mr. D., Mark Twain is dead—at least it is so reported."

"Is that so? Well, we have nothing against him—he never did any good. Publish an apparently friendly obituary of him—and say at the end that we are pained to have to state that for many years he gained his livelihood by the nefarious practice of robbing graveyards. That will be sufficient—I have already dished *him* up in a column editorial about his imbecile article upon the 'Cuban Patriot.'"

I said: "Mr. D., I beg pardon for mentioning it, but *I* am that Mark Twain to whose remains you propose to give a unique and pleasing interest, and I am not dead."

"Oh, you are the person, are you?—and you are not dead? Well, I am sorry, but I cannot help the matter. The obituary must be published. We are not responsible for your eccentricities; you *could* have been dead if you had chosen—nobody hindered you. The obituary is fair game, for whatever is Rumor to another paper is Fact to the *Sun*. And now that you are here handy, I will interview you. Please to give me the details of any aggravated or unnatural crimes you may have committed."

INTERVIEWING

The Interviewer. (Ital cap.

I found the editor of
the New York Sun throned
in his sanctum. He had
his brimless cap on — his
thinking cap, he terms it, &
well he may, for many an
exquisite fancy has it hatched
out in its time. ~~XXXH~~ He was
steeped in meditation. He
was arranging in his mind
a series of those articles for
~~the~~ his next day's paper which
have made the Sun fa-
mous in the land & a
welcome visitor in every
cultivated home circle
upon the continent —
interesting murders, with
all the toothsome partic-

ulars; libels upon such men & women as
have deserved the at-
tention by being promi-
nently blameless; aggra-
vated cases of incest, with
~~improv~~ improving & elevating details; prize
fights, elucidated with felicitously descriptive
technicalities; elaborate
histories of executions,
assassinations & se-
ductions; zealous de-
fences of Reddy the Blacksmith & other persecuted
patrons of the Sun who
chancets stumble into misfortune.
A high & noble thing it is
to be the chief editor of a
great metropolitan two-
cent journal & mould the
opinions of the washer-
women & achieve the ap-

"INTERVIEWING THE INTERVIEWER" (1870).

THE STRAIGHT INTERVIEW was a controversial new form of reporting in the 1870s, likened by one reader to the "interview" of Prometheus by vultures. To make up an interview was to play very rough indeed. Mark Twain was simply practicing the gentle art of "having a man for breakfast," as newspaper sensationalism was known in the West.

Charles A. Dana was just settling into his long career of running the New York Sun *when Mark Twain pounced on the "almost godlike" editor in January 1870. Dana was already a formidable journalist with friendships that Mark Twain must have envied. Before the Civil War, Dana's social circle had been the literary Transcendentalists of New England. His skill and sound judgment as a reporter led to his appointment as an Assistant Secretary of War under Abraham Lincoln. Only in a fictional interview was Mark Twain going to match wits with this man and leave the impression that the journalist was a sleazy liar.*

Dana's dream was to design a paper for working-class New Yorkers. His masthead read, "The Sun Shines for All— Price Two Cents." There is little chance that the publication of Mark Twain's satire would have been bad for this business. Dana's paper prospered in New York, absorbing the bare-knuckle press criticism of the day. This editor proudly traded on human interest and sensationalism. "I have always felt that whatever the Divine Providence permitted to occur I was not too proud to print," Dana said. His mortal sin was surely political for Mark Twain. The Sun *featured the scandals of the Grant Administration, tarnishing a hero that Mark Twain was ever-ready to defend with his pen.*

Mark Twain's "imbecile article" about Cuba also led him to square off with Dana. Clemens had written that article for his own Buffalo Express *and published it on Christmas day, 1869. This was a cry of outrage against both the Spanish government and the Cubans fighting for the colony's freedom. "Both sides massacre their prisoners," Mark Twain said, in*

warming to his subject, "a happy majority of both sides are
fantastic in costumes, grotesque in manner, half civilized,
unwashed, ignorant, bigoted, selfish, base, cruel, brutal, swag-
gering, plantation-burning semi-devils." Dana backed the
insurgents and started the New Year with an editorial to set
Mark Twain straight: "It is false that the Cubans are half-
civilized, ignorant, brutal, swaggering semi-devils. We have
known them long and well; and gentlemen of better principles,
higher honor, more genuine cultivation, more civilized and
refined manners, cannot be found in any country." Certainly
Samuel Clemens should not be their model, Dana sniffed, a
man "dressed to appear as a clown in the ring." In returning
the compliment that January with "Interviewing the
Interviewer," Mark Twain was staying in fighting trim. He
kept this manuscript out of print, evidently concluding that
enough was enough.

On Mark Twain's measurement of the size of Dana's ego
and tall tales in obituaries, the editor did have the last word.
After nearly three decades of leading a paper that touched
every cultural and political struggle of his time, he saw to it
that this was his own obituary, in its entirety, in 1897:
"CHARLES ANDERSON DANA, Editor of THE SUN,
died yesterday afternoon."

*　*　*

MARK TWAIN KNEW that America was a nation of small
towns, that most Americans got their news from a local editor,
and that the number and diversity of papers increased every
year. With the consolidation of media in our day, this may
seem like a golden age. It was not for Mark Twain, who liked
to compose curses on the press that were suitable for small
towns as well as large cities, upstart papers as well as old
mastheads. In an address to the Hartford Monday Evening
Club in 1873 he said

　　It seems to me that just in the ratio that our newspapers

increase, our morals decay. The more newspapers the
worse morals. Where we have one newspaper that does
good, I think that we have fifty that do harm. We ought
to look upon the establishment of a newspaper of the
average pattern in a virtuous village as a calamity.

Mark Twain spoke these words to the Evening Club and
was often a public scourge to journalists. But he had the habit
of protesting too much. He did not behave like a man who had
put the devil press behind him, or even wished to break its
embrace. Mark Twain was forever combing the news columns
for material and swapping stories with journalists. In letters
in The Bancroft Library from the 1870s we find him frantic
because a clipping he wanted to read from Dana's Sun *was*
missing from an envelope. Mark Twain even had a "shouting
good time" dining at Dana's home. Mark Twain's sermons on
the press drifted into bragging about his own newspaper sins.
As he told his Hartford club: "I know from personal experi-
ence, the proneness of journalists to lie. I once started a pecu-
liar and picturesque fashion of lying, myself, on the Pacific
coast, and it is not dead there to this day."

As every student of Mark Twain knows, he was always
enlightening but rarely consistent on the grave questions of
Victorian America. On race and politics, peace and war, God
and the hereafter, he felt his way along with contradictions and
shocks for the audience that wanted a tame funny man. If there
was a Mark Twain who could hold a steady course as press
critic, he emerged when foreigners attacked American journal-
ism. Only scholars have seen the essay that follows, aimed at
the British poet and critic Matthew Arnold. Mark Twain had
these words set in type by a prototype of the Paige typesetter,
the machine that would help him towards bankruptcy, but he
did not publish them. This private reflection went as far as
Mark Twain would go in showing his affection for the ram-
bunctious journalism that contributed so much to his view of
the world:

The American Press

> Goethe says somewhere that "the thrill of awe"—that is to say, REVERENCE—"is the best thing humanity has." —MATTHEW ARNOLD.

> I should say that if one were searching for the best means to efface and kill in a whole nation the discipline of respect, one could not do better than take the American newspapers. —MATTHEW ARNOLD.

RESPONSE.

MR. ARNOLD JUDGED of our newspapers without stopping to consider what their mission was. He judged them from the European standpoint; and he could not have found an improperer one to judge an American newspaper from.

Take the most important function of a journal in any country, and what is it? To furnish the news? No—that is secondary. Its first function is the guiding and moulding of public opinion, the propagating of national feeling, and pride in the national name—in a word, the keeping the people in love with their country and its institutions, and shielded from the allurements of alien and inimical systems. If this premiss be granted—and certainly none will deny it—Mr. Arnold mistook for a flaw in our journalism a thing which is not a flaw at all, but its supremest merit.

In Constantinople there was a newspaper some years ago—a kind of a newspaper—and it may be there yet, though the climate was pretty rugged for it. That little paper could shout as vigorously as it wanted to when it was praising our Holy Established Church of Mahomet; or lauding the sublimities of the Sultan's character and virtues; or describing how the nation adored the dust he walked upon; or what grief and dismay swept the land when he was ill for a couple of days; and it could branch out and tell tales and invent stories—pious, guileful, goody-goody nursery tales showing how odious and awful are all forms of human liberty, and how holy and healthy and beautiful is the only right government, the only true and beneficent government for human beings—a despotism; a despotism invented by God, conferred directly by the grace of God, nourished, watched over, by God; and to criticise which, is to utter blasphemy. It was working its function, you see—keeping the people's ideas in the right shape. But there were things which it might not shout about—things concerning which it must be judiciously blind, and deaf, and most respectfully quiet. Now would you look for a joke, or lightsome chaff, or a frivolous remark, in that journalistic hearse? You would be disappointed; it was not the place for it. An Arctic gravity, decorum, reverence, was its appointed gait: for the devil's aversion to holy water is a light matter compared with a despot's dread of a newspaper that laughs. Does this description describe the Turkish journal? It does. Does it describe the Russian journal? It does. Does it describe the German journal? It does. Does it describe the English journal? With unimportant modifications, it does. If the flies in a spider's web had a journal, would it describe that one, too? It would. By the language of that journal you would get the idea that to a fly's mind—a fly in a web—there is nothing in the world that is quite so winsome, and gracious, and provocative of gushing and affectionate reverence, as a great gilt-backed, steel-fanged, well-intrenched spider.

The chief function of an English journal is that of all other journals the world over: it must keep the public eye fixed admiringly upon certain things, and keep it diligently diverted from certain others. For instance, it must keep the public eye fixed admiringly upon the glories of England, a processional splendor stretching its receding line down the hazy vistas of time, with the mellowed lights of a thousand years glinting from its banners; and it must keep it diligently diverted from the fact that all these glories were for the enrichment and aggrandizement of the petted and privileged few, at cost of the blood and sweat and poverty of the unconsidered masses who achieved them but might not enter in and partake of them. It must keep the public eye fixed in loving and awful reverence upon the throne, as a sacred thing, and diligently divert it from the fact that no throne was ever set up by the unhampered vote of a majority of any nation, and that hence no throne exists that has a right to exist, and no symbol of it, flying from any flagstaff, is righteously entitled to wear any device but the skull and cross-bones of that kindred industry which differs from royalty only business-wise—merely as retail differs from wholesale. It must keep the citizen's eye fixed in reverent docility upon that curious invention of machine politics, an Established Church, and upon that bald contradiction of common justice, a hereditary nobility; and diligently divert it from the fact that the one damns him if he doesn't wear its collar, and robs him under the gentle name of taxation whether he wears it or not, and the other gets all the honors while he does all the work.

Dear me, the dignity, the austerity, the petrified solemnity which Mr. Arnold admired and estimated as a merit in the English press, is not a merit, it is inseparable from the situation. Necessarily, journalism under a monarchy can do its hard duty and perform its grotesque function with but one mien—a graveyard gravity of countenance: to laugh would expose the whole humbug. For the very existence of a sham depends upon this cast-iron law—that it shall not be laughed at. And its prosperity depends upon this other law—that men shall speak of it with bated breath, respectfully, reverently: according to the gospel of Matthew Arnold and Goethe the poet.

Mr. Arnold, with his trained eye and intelligent obser-

& protector of human liberty —
even as the other thing is the creator,
nurse, & steadfast protector of
all forms of human slavery,
bodily & mental.

I believe it is our irreverent
press which has laughed away,
one by one, what remained of
our inherited minor shams & delusions & serfages after the Revolution, & made us the only really
free people that has yet existed
in the earth; & I believe we shall
remain free, utterly free & unassailably free, until some alien
critic with sugared speech shall
persuade our journalism to forsake its scoffing ways & serve
itself up on the innocuous European

TWO PAGES FROM THE MANUSCRIPT OF

plan. Our press has done a worthy work; is doing a worthy work; & so, though one should prove to me — a thing easily within the possibilities — that its faults are abundant & over-abundant, I should still say, no matter: so long as it still possesses that supreme virtue in journalism, an active & discriminating irreverence, it will be entitled to hold itself the most valuable press, the most wholesome press, & the most puissant force for the nurture & protection of human freedom that either hemisphere has yet produced since the printer's art set itself the tedious & disheartening task of righting the wrongs of men.

To gather into a sheaf the random

"THE AMERICAN PRESS" (1888).

vation, ought to have perceived that the very quality which he so regretfully missed from our press—respectfulness, reverence—is exactly the thing which would make our press useless to us if it had it—rob it of the very thing which differentiates it from all other journalism on the globe and makes it distinctively and preciously American. Its frank and cheerful irreverence is by all odds the most valuable quality it possesses. For its mission—overlooked by Mr. Arnold—is to stand guard over a nation's liberties, not its humbugs and shams. And so it must be armed with ridicule, not reverence. If during fifty years you could impose the blight of English journalistic solemnity and timid respect for stately shams upon our press, it is within the possibilities that the republic would perish; and if during fifty years you could expose the stately and moss-grown shams of Europe to the fire of a flouting and scoffing press like ours, it is almost a moral certainty that monarchy and its attendant crimes would disappear from Christendom.

Well, the charge is, that our press has but little of that old-world quality, reverence. Let us be candidly grateful that this is so. With its limited reverence it at least reveres the things which this nation reveres, as a rule, and that is sufficient: what other people revere is fairly and properly matter of light importance to us. Our press does not reverence kings, it does not reverence so-called nobilities, it does not reverence established ecclesiastical slaveries, it does not reverence laws which rob a younger son to fatten an elder one, it does not reverence any fraud or sham or infamy, howsoever old or rotten or holy, which sets one citizen above his neighbor by accident of birth; it does not reverence any law or custom, howsoever old or decayed or sacred, which shuts against the best man in the land the best place in the land and the divine right to prove property and go up and occupy it. In the sense of the poet Goethe —that meek idolater of provincial three-carat royalty and nobility—our press is certainly bankrupt in the "thrill of awe"—otherwise reverence: reverence for nickle-plate and brummagem. Let us sincerely hope that this fact will remain a fact forever: for to my mind a discriminating irreverence is the creator and protector of human liberty— even as the other thing is the creator, nurse, and steadfast protector of all forms of human slavery, bodily and mental.

I believe it is our irreverent press which has laughed away, one by one, what remained of our inherited minor shams and delusions and serfages after the Revolution, and made us the only really free people that has yet existed in the earth; and I believe we shall remain free, utterly free and unassailably free, until some alien critic with sugared speech shall persuade our journalism to forsake its scoffing ways and serve itself up on the innocuous European plan. Our press has done a worthy work; is doing a worthy work; and so, though one should prove to me—a thing easily within the possibilities—that its faults are abundant and over-abundant, I should still say, no matter: so long as it still possesses that supreme virtue in journalism, an active and discriminating irreverence, it will be entitled to hold itself the most valuable press, the most wholesome press, and the most puissant force for the nurture and protection of human freedom that either hemisphere has yet produced since the printer's art set itself the tedious and dishearten- ing task of righting the wrongs of men.

To gather into a sheaf the random argument which I have left scattered behind me over the field: I take issue with the old-world doctrine of Goethe and Mr. Arnold, that reverence has but one office—to elevate. It has more than one. There is a reverence which elevates, there is a rever- ence which degrades. To pay reverence to a man who has done sublime work for his race and his generation, even though he were born as poor and nameless as that plodding German who invented the movable types, and so by his single might lifted a flaming intellectual sun into a zenith where mental midnight had reigned before, elevates him who pays it; but to pay reverence to a mere king, or prince, or duke, or any other empty accident, must degrade and does degrade any man or nation that pays it. And I am not able to believe that any intelligent man has ever lived within this superstition-dissipating century—even Goethe—who paid it and was not secretly ashamed of it.

"THE AMERICAN PRESS" is the complementary piece to the thinking about graduation that Mark Twain was doing in the summer of 1888. At age 52, Yale University had awarded him his first honorary degree (his first degree of any kind) in June. Clemens reminded Yale's president that Matthew Arnold had no use for the American "funny men" but that Yale's honor showed that the humorist's trade was worthy: "the deriding of shams, the exposure of pretentious falsities, the laughing of stupid superstitions out of existence." It was a short step to find in another encounter with Arnold "that supreme virtue of journalism, an active and discriminating irreverence." Mark Twain had graduated to a fuller understanding of his life's work.

For all the ink that Mark Twain shed to put Arnold in his place (this is but one example of many) the two men got on well socially. Arnold's question to the Reverend Edwin Pond Parker—a Hartford friend of Clemens's—after meeting Mark Twain there in 1883, was, "And is he never serious?" Parker's answer to the British visitor applies to Mark Twain's wide swings of emotion on the press: "Mr. Arnold, he is the most serious man in the world." Mark Twain's ability to see shams entwined with privilege, and liberating plain speech in a democracy, gave him a foundation of loyalty to the American press, no matter his unending quarrels with journalists.

T. C. L.

APPENDIX

[The following text is incomplete, both at the beginning and the end, but it is all that survives of the remarks Mark Twain made to the Hartford Monday Evening Club on 31 March 1873. The title was assigned by Albert Bigelow Paine, the author's official biographer, who published it in 1923.]

[*License of the Press*]

... all consequences. It has scoffed at religion till it has made scoffing popular. It has defended official criminals, on party pretexts, until it has created a United States Senate which is incapable of determining what crime against law and the dignity of their own body *is* they are so morally blind, and it has made light of dishonesty till we have as a result a Congress which contracts to work for a certain sum and then deliberately steals additional wages out of the public pocket and is pained and surprised that anybody should worry about a little thing like that.

I am putting all this odious state of things upon the newspaper, and I believe it belongs there—chiefly, at any rate. It is a free press—a press that is more than free—a press which is licensed to say any infamous thing it chooses about a private or a public man, or advocate any outrageous doctrine it pleases. It is tied in NO way. The public opinion which *should* hold it in bounds it has itself degraded to its own level. There are laws to protect the freedom of the press's speech, but none that are worth anything to protect the people from the press. A libel suit simply brings the plaintiff before a vast newspaper court to be tried before the law tries him, and reviled and ridiculed without mercy. The touchy Charles Reade can sue English newspapers, and get verdicts; he would soon change his tactics here; the papers (backed by a public well taught by themselves) would soon teach him that it is better to suffer any amount of misrepresentation than go into our courts with a libel suit and make himself the laughing stock of the community.

It seems to me that just in the ratio that our newspapers increase, our morals decay. The more newspapers the worse morals. Where we have one newspaper that does good, I think we have fifty that do harm. We *ought* to look upon the establishment of a newspaper of the average pattern in a virtuous village as a calamity.

The difference between the tone and conduct of newspapers today and those of 30 or 40 years ago is *very* noteworthy and very sad—I mean the average newspaper (for they had bad ones then, too.) In those days the average newspaper was the champion of right and morals, and it dealt conscientiously in the truth. It is not the case now. The other day a reputable New York daily had an editorial defending the salary steal and justifying it on the ground that Congressmen were not paid enough—as if that were an all-sufficient excuse for stealing. That editorial put the matter in a new and perfectly satisfactory light with many a leather-headed reader, without a doubt. It has become a sarcastic proverb that a thing must be true if you saw it in a newspaper. That is the opinion intelligent people have of that lying vehicle, in a nutshell. But the trouble is that the stupid people—who constitute the grand overwhelming majority of this and all other nations—*do* believe and *are* moulded and convinced by what they get out of a newspaper, and there is where the harm lies.

Among us, the newspaper is a tremendous power. It can make or mar any man's reputation. It has perfect freedom to call the best man in the land a fraud and a thief, and he is destroyed beyond help. Whether Mr. Colfax is a liar or not can never be ascertained, now—but he will rank as one till the day of his death—for the newspapers have so doomed him. Our newspapers—*all* of them, without exception— glorify the Black Crook and make it an opulent success—

they could have killed it dead with one broadside of contemptuous silence if they had wanted to. "Days' Doings" and "Police Gazettes" flourish in the land unmolested by the law, because the *virtuous* newspapers long ago nurtured up a public laxity that loves indecency and never cares whether laws are administered or not.

In the newspapers of the West you can use the *editorial voice* in the editorial columns, to defend any wretched and injurious dogma you please by paying a dollar a line for it.

Nearly all newspapers foster Rozensweigs and kindred criminals and send victims to them by opening their columns to their advertisements. You all know that.

In the Foster murder case the New York papers made a weak pretense of upholding the hands of the governor and urging the people to sustain him in standing firmly by the law; but they printed a whole page of sickly, maudlin appeals to his clemency as a paid advertisement. And I suppose they would have published enough pages of abuse of the governor to destroy his efficiency as a public official to the end of his term if anybody had come forward and paid them for it—as an advertisement. The newspaper that obstructs the law on a trivial pretext, for money's sake is a dangerous enemy to the public weal.

That awful power, the public opinion of a nation, is created in America by a horde of ignorant, self-complacent simpletons who failed at ditching and shoemaking and fetched up in journalism on their way to the poorhouse. I am personally acquainted with hundreds of journalists, and the opinion of the majority of them would not be worth tuppence in private, but when they speak in print, it is the *newspaper* that is talking (the pigmy scribe is not visible) and *then* their utterances shake the community like the thunders of prophecy.

I know from personal experience, the proneness of journalists to lie. I once started a peculiar and picturesque fashion of lying, myself, on the Pacific coast, and it is not dead there to this day. Whenever I hear of a shower of blood and frogs combined, in California, or a sea-serpent found in some desert, there, or a cave frescoed with diamonds and emeralds (*always* found by an Injun who died before he could finish telling where it was,) I say to myself I am the father of this child—I have got to answer for this lie. And habit is everything—to this day I am liable to lie if I don't watch all the time.

The license of the press has scorched every individual of us in our time, I make no doubt. Poor Stanley was a very god, in England, his praises in every man's mouth. But nobody said anything about his lectures—they were charitably quiet on that head, and were content to praise his higher virtues. But our papers tore the poor creature limb from limb and scattered the fragments from Maine to California—merely because he couldn't lecture good. His prodigious achievement in Africa goes for naught—the man is pulled down and utterly destroyed—but *still* the persecution follows him as relentlessly from city to city and from village to village as if he had committed some bloody and detestable crime. Bret Harte was suddenly snatched out of obscurity by our papers and throned in the clouds— all the editors in the land stood out in the inclement weather and adored him through their telescopes and swung their hats till they wore them out and then borrowed more; and the first time his family fell sick and in his trouble and harassment he ground out a rather flat article in place of another heathen Chinee, that hurrahing host said Why this man's a fraud—and then they began to reach up there for him. And they got him, too, and fetched him down, and walked over him, and rolled him in the mud, and tarred and feathered him, and then set him up for a target and have been heaving dirt at him ever since. The result is that the man has had only just 19 engagements to lecture this year, and the audiences have been so scattering, too, that he has never discharged a sentence yet that hit two people at the same time. The man is ruined—never can get up again. And yet he is a person who has great capabilities, and might have accomplished great things for our literature and for himself if he had had a happier chance. And he made the mistake, too, of doing a pecuniary kindness for a starving beggar of our guild—one of the journalistic shoe-maker class—and that beggar made it his business as soon as he got back to San Francisco, to publish 4 columns of exposures of crimes committed by his benefactor, the least of which ought to make any decent man blush. The press that admitted that stuff to its columns had too much license.

In a town in Michigan, I declined to dine with an editor who was drunk, and he said in his paper that my lecture was profane, indecent, and calculated to encourage intemperance. And yet that man never heard it. It might have reformed him if he had.

A Detroit paper once said that I was in the constant habit of beating my wife and that I still kept this recreation up although I had crippled her for life and she was no longer able to keep out of my way when I came home in my usual frantic frame of mind. Now scarcely the half of that was true. Perhaps I ought to have sued that man for libel—but I knew better. All the papers in America—with a few creditable exceptions—would have found out then, to *their* satisfaction that I was a wife beater, and they would have given it a pretty general airing, too.

Why *I* have published vicious libels upon people, *myself*—and ought to have been hanged before my time for it, too—if I *do* say it myself that shouldn't.

But I will not continue these remarks. I have a sort of vague general idea that there is too much liberty of the press in this country, and that through the absence of all wholesome restraint the newspaper has become in a large degree a national *curse*, and will probably damn the Republic yet.

There *are* some excellent virtues in newspapers, some powers that wield vast influences for good; and I could have told all about these things, and glorified them exhaustively—but that would have left you gentlemen nothing to say. It is conceded that it is....

For The Friends of The Bancroft Library
This book was designed and printed by Marianne Hinckle
AÑO NUEVO ISLAND PRESS.

Words for this keepsake were composed in William Caslon's
Old Style Roman at Hillside Press. Offset lithography by
On Paper, Inc.; letterpress jacket printed at Hillside Press
with Caravan ornaments by W. A. Dwiggins.